IMAGES OF SCOTLAND

AROUND
CRIEFF AND
STRATHEARN

IMAGES OF SCOTLAND

AROUND
CRIEFF AND
STRATHEARN

COLIN MAYALL

TEMPUS

*I dedicate this book to my late son, Richard P. Mayall,
sadly missed by all his family.*

Frontispiece: The Range, at Ardvreck School, in 1902.

First published 2004

Tempus Publishing Limited
The Mill, Brimscombe Port,
Stroud, Gloucestershire, GL5 2QG
www.tempus-publishing.com

British Library Cataloguing in Publication Data.
A catalogue record for this book is available from the British Library.

ISBN 0 7524 2797 0

Typesetting and origination by Tempus Publishing Limited.
Printed in Great Britain.

Contents

	Acknowledgements	6
	Introduction	7
one	Agriculture	9
two	Sport	17
three	Buildings and Bridges	25
four	Rover Moot	55
five	Streets of Crieff	61
six	A Strathearn Miscellany	69
seven	Railways	111
eight	Crieff Hydro	123

Acknowledgements

Without the kind assistance of so many local Strathearn people, this book would not have been possible. My thanks go to Joan Longden for availing me of her superb postcard collection; to David Cowan, author and scientific investigator, for photographs taken by himself over the years; to Bill Tracey, local sportsman, for his input on football in Strathearn; to Margaret and John Forrest for allowing me the use of their personal collection depicting life on the farm in Strathearn; to John Hughes, author and whisky expert, for bits and pieces; and to war historian Bob Holsman, for advising me on the various military pictures I have included. I also extend my thanks to the many others who paused to answer my queries and point me in the right direction.

Drummond Street, Muthill, in around 1900.

Introduction

Crieff, regarded as the capital of Strathearn, lies in the heart of Scotland, virtually equidistant from towns of the east and those of the west. The name is said to be derived from the Gaelic *craobh*, meaning 'amongst the trees', although one school of thought suggests it comes from the Gaelic meaning the haunch or side of a hill. It was for these geographic reasons that the town became the scene of one of the largest cattle markets in Britain during the latter part of the eighteenth century. The Tryst brought some 30,000 highland cattle to the town for the Michaelmas Market. For a brief period each year Crieff became one of the country's most important money centres, as the covered wagons from Edinburgh arrived with the newfangled paper money to exchange for the gold of the drovers or cattlemen. Changing economic circumstances saw the Tryst move to Falkirk at the end of the century. It was fortuitous that its demise happened to coincide with the rapid rise in the hand-loom weaving cottage industry throughout rural Scotland. By 1851 about one-third of the working population was involved in the spinning and weaving of linen and cotton. The Crieff Weavers' Society, founded in 1768, was the first of its kind in Strathearn. The neighbouring towns and villages of Comrie, Auchterarder, Muthill and Fowlis Wester were later offshoots of this parent body.

Although hand-loom weaving was the main occupation of the towns of Strathearn for nearly 100 years, it declined rapidly after the 1820s. It lasted longer here than elsewhere in Scotland, but by the 1870s it was virtually finished. Once again, fate seemed to play a hand. The opening of the Crieff Junction Line connecting the town with the Scottish Central Railway (the main north/south artery) at Gleneagles in 1856 brought the town into touch with the outside world. In 1866 a direct connection with the county town of Perth was opened with the new Crieff and Methven Junction Railway. Such was the interest that it is reputed that over 1,000 passengers in three trains left the town on the first day. It is assumed that most of them managed to return!

The arrival of the railway coincided with the opening of the Strathearn Hydropathic Hotel in 1868. The Hydro, as it is more familiarly known, was a purpose-built structure, having some forty bedrooms set amidst fifteen acres of ground. It is now one of the largest and most successful hotels of its type in the country. Still in the private ownership of the family who founded it all those years ago, it has expanded enormously to provide the many facilities expected by today's family holidaymaker.

The railways also brought an influx of new residents to the town and area. Large stone-built villas sprang up on the gentle slopes north of the town, and many of the clay and stone 'biggins' of an earlier era were demolished, whilst stone slates replaced traditional heather thatch on the weavers' cottages of Mitchell and Millar Street. Analysis of the early census returns shows that many of these incomers had made money in the burgeoning industries of Scotland's Central Belt or, as one can jalouse from house names, many new residents had worked in the tea plantations of the Far East. Strathearn – and Crieff, in particular – became a popular destination for the Victorian and Edwardian holidaymaker, and early guide books refer to it as the 'Montpelier of the North'! Agriculture was predominant in the rural areas, whilst in Crieff tanning, papermaking, sawmilling and power-loom weaving all gave employment to the expanding population.

Although this book deals with the post 1850s, especially in its pictorial content, it would be totally remiss not to draw the reader's attention to times prior to this. Strathearn was the ancient Pictish Kingdom of Fortren, and Forteviot beside the Earn was the first capital of what we now call Scotland. The Romans erected a massive camp at Braco, some ten miles south of Crieff, and created a chain of forts along the Gask Ridge bisecting the Strath. These forts are now regarded as the oldest Roman frontier in Europe. The ubiquitous standing stones in the fields of Strathearn are ancient reminders that the area was peopled by Neolithic tribesman as far back as 3,000BC.

The illustrations in this book depict various facets of life in this most picturesque part of Perthshire. Ours is a vibrant society with a rich past. Much, of course, has changed with the passage of time, but equally, much has not!

one
Agriculture

Farm transport. The Horne sisters off on a visit dressed in their Sunday best in around 1916.

Harvesting with binders in the 1930s. Before the Second World War, mechanisation on the farm had not really arrived. This is Dornock Farm near Crieff.

Right: Wartime on the farm. Strathearn was an area where families from war-struck areas of the country, particularly in the west around Glasgow and Clydebank, were decanted for their own safety. Some of these visitors are shown lending a hand at harvest time at Dornock, about 1942.

Below: A common scene around Strathearn farms was the stallion arriving to perform his duties. This 1931 scene at Dornock shows the drayman tending the champion Percheron from that year's Royal Highland Show.

Above: Life was not all work, and here entertainment was being provided in the fields of the farm. This 1920s scene shows a 'turnip thinning competition', organised by the local young farmers, and which attracted considerable interest.

Below: Beehives on the farm in the 1920s. Farms had to be diverse in the early part of the twentieth century. Here are the Dornock beehives, which provided an additional food source.

Safety on the farm. The 1940s saw a concerted Government effort to introduce safety, health and welfare measures to the farming community. This carefully posed picture shows the local policeman or fire officer pointing to the workers with pipes in their mouths. The immediate post-war period on the farm was very much horse-orientated, with tractors still a comparative rarity.

Above: Milnab Mill, now the Park Manor Flats, in 1903. Milnab Mill was a meal mill and stood until it was demolished to make way for the Park Manor Flats in the 1970s.

Left: Park Manor Flats, which replaced the Milnab Mill in the late1970s. Two blocks were built by the Perth builders A. & J. Stephen.

Opposite above: Strageath Mill. For many years the farming communities were served by a number of water-powered mills which provided meal and other products for local and distant consumption. Strageath Mill on the banks of the Earn, adjoining the site of a large Roman camp, still stands in part but is missing the wheel. This picture dates from the 1920s.

Situated virtually opposite Strathgeath on the other bank was Dornock Mill, demolished in the 1920s.

The Roman Bridge and Monzie Mill. On the edge of the village of Monzie was another mill, long since gone. Interestingly, the old bridge is referred to locally as the 'Roman Bridge', and is similar to the one spanning the nearby Barvick Burn to the west. Although the area was occupied by the Romans for some 200 years, the bridge appears to be of a much later construction.

Another meal mill which prospered for many years, the Dalvreck Mill, was owned and run by Robert Taylor, who also owned the mill at Bridgend. Local farmer Bob Simpson recalls that further up the Turret Burn there was an old meal mill at Greenend, with a timber mill close by which was destroyed by fire in the 1960s.

two

Sport

The first cricket team in Strathearn was founded in 1853 and played, as it still does, at the Bridgend to the south of the town. But the cricketers seemed somewhat nomadic and appeared to move around the area – matches were played at Duchlage, Perth Road, and also near the quaintly named Bogle House beside the old Hollybush Farm. According to the late George Ewing, the written records of Crieff Cricket Club were thrown away, and sadly we are now left with little evidence of a long and interesting sporting past.

Although the Cricket Section of Crieff Cricket and Rugby Club is now more the junior partner, it was not always the case. The 1968 team won the Perthshire Cup as well as the Perthshire League, against strong opposition. The county has numerous village teams and competition has over many decades been keen. The triumphant team included a number of well-known personalities. The late George Ewing, a cricketer of perhaps modest ability on the field, was outstanding in both administration and as an umpire. C.P. (Chick) Murphy, local businessman and stalwart of the club, gained a reputation as a bowler of some ability, whilst A.W. (Billy) Sinclair, farmer at nearby Fowlis, was a feared opponent not only on the cricket square but as a doughty rugby player with Perthshire Academicals. Wicket keeper Neilly Watters played behind the stumps for some four decades and, apart from claiming wickets a plenty, was an accomplished bat. Neil's talents extended into the football field, where his abilities as a goalie saw him gain glory with the local Vale of Earn when they won the Perthshire League in 1967/68. In the nineties the club enjoyed the all-round skills of the late Andrew Foster, a Yorkshireman and teacher at Ardvreck Preparatory School in Crieff. He was a prodigious bat and his elegant scoring style is sadly missed.

Above: Rugby in its early days, a game comparatively new to the Strath. A letter to the *Strathearn Herald* in 1985 regarding the origins of the game locally elucidated a number of responses. The late Robert Bain of Coldwells Road in Crieff mentioned that in the 1920s the former pupils of Morrisons Academy played as The Crieff Academical Club. Prior to the First World War, the school played both codes, rugby as well as football (soccer) and the same boy captained both teams. Mr Bain recounted that one Harold Paul was the outstanding sportsman of his day. Harold, who eventually played for Queens Park and Scotland, is recounted as playing rugby for the school in the morning and then slipping away to turn out for the Morrisonians at football in the afternoon against St Johnstone, scoring a couple of goals in the process and becoming something of a local hero. Rugby was played at Turret Bridge and the picture shows the former pupils' club, known as the Morrisonians, in season 1933/1934. Amongst the players are Bill Allan, former manager of the local Savings Bank, Tom Donaldson, well-known garage proprietor and businessman and R.G. Mickel, local solicitor and town clerk. In those days clubs such as the Morrisonians played a social rugby and were not involved in the modern–day high pressure league set-up that has changed the game.

Below: Rugby has changed. This informal gathering of Crieff Rugby Club, taken at their ground at the Braidhaugh about 1998, shows players and committee men about to depart for a tour of Majorca. Despite a hiccup in their fortunes in the late 1980s, the club has grown in strength with a broad base of support, and won the national Division VB Championship in season 2003/04. They changed their name to Crieff and Strathearn to indicate a less parochial base than previously. They run two senior teams and junior, midi and mini sections catering for all ages from eight years upwards. The club are the most cosmopolitan of local sporting outfits, having over the years attracted players from New Zealand, Australia, South Africa, Fiji, Ireland and even England. Indeed, three out of four of the last club captains have been Sassanachs!

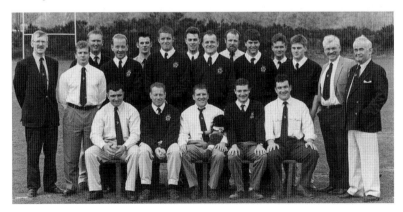

Above: Ardvreck Preparatory School, on the outskirts of Crieff, was founded in 1883 along the lines of the traditional English public school system. It always had a strong sporting tradition and this 1907 photograph by C.C. Foster shows the school's annual match with rivals Cargilfield, probably the oldest rugby action photograph in Strathearn.

Above left: The River Earn flows from Loch Earn in an easterly direction until it joins with the Tay below Perth. Renowned for both salmon and sea trout, the Earn has both private and club beats which provide excellent sport for both locals and visitors to the area. The Crieff Angling Club has a history stretching back to the 1880s, when it first saw light under the name 'The Crieff District Fishing Law Reform Association'. This is a mammoth 68lb salmon recovered dead from the water between Crieff and Comrie sometime in the 1960s by Willie Stewart of Crieff (pictured).

Above right: The Vale of Earn Perthshire League Champions, 1967/68, one of the best teams to come out of Crieff. Manager Bill Tracy, well-known local businessman and sports aficionado, managed the squad, captained by 'Fordie' Hunter. It included many who are still around the town today, including Ronnie McKay, Alec Brock, Sandy Neil and John Strachan. The team's great win over Lethem of Perth by 2-1 is still remembered by many. They went on to win the League title, defeating St Johns in the play off, played at Huntingtower. The following year Bill's boys reached the final of the Scottish Juvenile Cup and were more than a little unlucky to miss out on the title.

Crieff Highland Games in 1904. Still going strong after well over 100 years, the Crieff Annual Games is, for many locals, still the focal point of the summer. Apart from the usual athletics, heavies, piping and dancing, the organisers always endeavour to bring to the town a 'special attraction'. Here, in 1904, the crowd were being entertained by a 'military display'.

The Games in 1906. This somewhat congested scene of an Edwardian Games Day again seems to have a strong military content. Apart from the brass band, we can see a mounted display being performed by a cavalry regiment. The view is northwards, showing the existing station buildings over the wall from the Market Park.

This postcard of the 1906 Games shows that it was not all about military displays and gymnastics! A good sized crowd at the King Street end of the Market Park watch one of the heavies put the heavy shot. The 'trig' is not the modern circle, but a simple length of plank. Note the Edwardian deviation as one official sports a straw boater with his kilt!

A splendid line up at the Games in around 1900, depicting the athletes, cyclists and pipers in front of the old stand, which was a feature of the Market Park. Sadly, it burnt down some forty or so years ago and its portable equivalent comes and goes in the span of a week!

Right: A Crieff highlander of yesteryear. A McFarlane studio portrait of a young Crieff man displaying medals which may have been won at the games for piping or dancing.

Below: Bowling remains one of the most popular pastimes in the area. This picture, taken about 1900, shows a game on the Coldwells Green. The Crieff Club still play their games here and it is probably the oldest existing sports club in the area. Other facilities are at the Hydro. The public green in Millar Street closed in 2004.

Crieff Golf Club has a modern clubhouse and two courses situated on the old Ferntower Estate. This 1930s picture of the old bungalow-style clubhouse reflects a time when car parking was not an issue.

Golf House, Dornoch, Crieff

An elegant Edwardian view of Dornock Golf Course. Prior to moving to Ferntower, Crieff Golf Club played at Dornock, near Highlandman. Players would take the train from Crieff to cover the short distance to the course, which was within walking distance of Highlandman Station. The clubhouse is still there but is now a private residence.

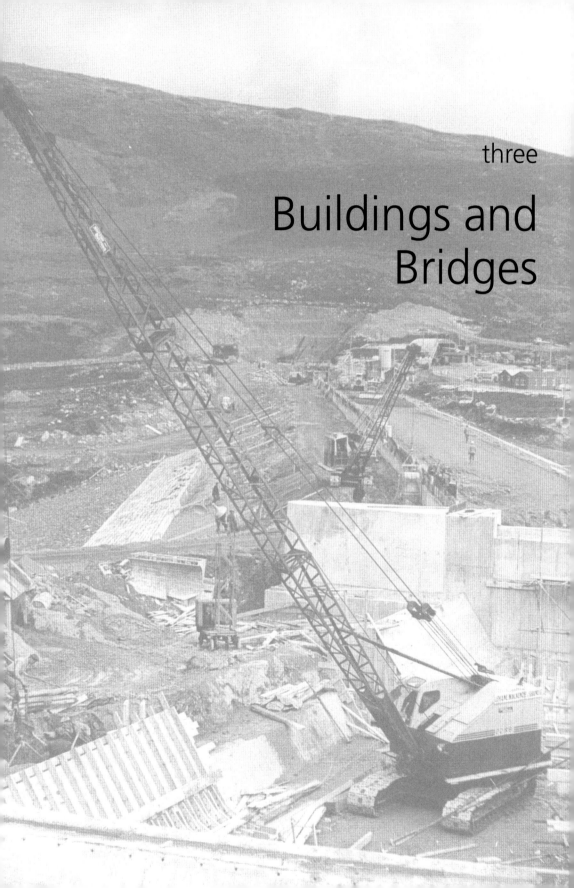

three

Buildings and Bridges

Visitors to Crieff will always find a Charming Selection of Novelties at

SCRIMGEOUR'S

The Fashion House, CRIEFF

Above left: Scrimgeour's Corner in Crieff. This landmark in Crieff was destroyed by fire in 1977. Scrimgeour's had been a draper's in the town since about 1815. The building shown in the picture was constructed in 1916, rebuilt on the original site, and was, despite its somewhat severe architectural lines, a noted landmark in the town. The brothers Alec and John Scrimgeour, who had founded the business, sold out in 1899. The name, however, was retained. The new owners John Robertson and David Halley had been apprentices in the original enterprise and built it from a solid base. To quote the *Strathearn Herald* of 22 January 1977, 'The building at that time (1899) was much larger than it was before Tuesday's disastrous fire. It jutted out to where the pavement railing is now and made a right-angle block at the corner, making life somewhat difficult for the occasional car or horse-drawn carriage.' The *Herald* relates a tale told to them by Hamish Halley, son of the aforementioned David:

> I remember when the building was being reconstructed. I was a wee lad of seven and walked the 'tight rope' along the rafters. Before the work started my father and Mr Robertson had offered to sell that chunk of land on the corner to the Council, so that the place could be rebuilt. There was an almighty row in the Council over the matter because one Councillor said it would enable vehicles to travel at the speed of ten miles an hour and more. One of the Councillors said, 'Who the hell would want to travel at more than ten miles per hour?'

After the fire, the building was demolished and for many years 'Scrimgeour's Corner' was a real eyesore, before eventually being replaced by a contemporary purpose-built block of flats.

Above right: The new 'Scrimgeour's' – the modern flats which rose from the ashes of the old store.

Opposite below: Looking over to Rhuad mhor, a scene prior to the raising of the waters, looking from the west bank over to the old shooting lodge.

Above: Rhuad mhor. The Murrays of Ochtertyre were one of the leading families in the Strath for many years. Their lands stretched northwards from their Georgian home above Ochtertyre to the tranquil shores of Loch Turret, nestling at the foot of Ben Chonzie. The family had a delightful shooting lodge known as Rhuad mhor. This charming building in the Scots vernacular with turrets and crow-stepped gables was demolished in the 1950s as a consequence of the new dam, which raised water levels to their present level. Local resident Iain Somerville recalls playing in the empty property before the dozers moved in and recalls that the stairway to the tower featured purpose-made Morris wallpaper depicting the wildlife of the area.

The construction of the Loch Turret dam in the 1950s. This aerial view shows work proceeding on the dam, which raised the water level dramatically and sent the waters tumbling by pipeline to feed the new petro chemical industries and homes around Grangemouth.

Visited by Queen Victoria and admired for its elegance and opulence, Abercairney, like so many of the large homes of the period, succumbed to the ravages of time and was demolished in the 1950s.

INCHBRAKIE HOUSE.

Once the home of the Graemes of Inchbrakie, kin people of the great Duke of Montrose, the old mansion is long since gone, with little trace remaining. (Etching kindly lent by Grace Cuthbert of Comrie)

Fern Tower, Crieff

JV 2463

Ferntower House, a distinctive though small eighteenth-century traditional house, described in the 1911 articles of sale as a 'Scottish gentleman's house in the Palladian style', was for many years the home of the Campbell Preston family. Ann Campbell Preston married the distinguished soldier Sir David Baird, whose memory is encapsulated in the striking Baird's Monument on Tom na Chastel as well as the small village of Madderty St Davids between Crieff and Perth. At one time the estate encompassed over 3,300 acres of land, including the farms of Crieffvechter, Colony, Greenhead, Peathills, Tomaknock, Laker, Parkside, Westbank, Muirmouth, Cargates, Woodburn, Newraw, Muirend and Craig, as well as the Callum's Hill Quarry! The house and estate were sold in 1911 and the grounds surrounding the old house were transformed into what is now Crieff Golf Course. The house itself fell into decay and was demolished, or more specifically blown up, by the army in the 1950s.

Opposite below: Abruchill Castle, Comrie. For three centuries it was the seat of the Campbells of Aber or Abruchill, who were connected to the Campbells of Lawers. The castle was built in 1602 but has been altered over the years and survived a bad fire in the 1990s. The family were staunch Presbyterians and Whigs, 'when most of the gentry of Strathearn were Episcopalians or Popish Jacobites'! (Revd William Marshall, *Historic Scenes of Perthshire*, Oliphant 1880)

Above: Strowan Bridge, now demolished, and replaced with a contemporary modern structure, from downstream.

Abruchill Castle, Comrie

COMRIE: THE OLD BRIDGE.

The old bridge at Dalginross, Comrie, another bridge to have disappeared. Dalginross was for many years a village within a village, where many of the hand-loom weavers plied their trade.

The new bridge at Dalginross, which replaced the original in the early part of the last century.

Strowan House, another of the elegant family houses of the area, no longer standing. It was demolished and replaced with a modern substitute about half a century ago.

Strowan Bridge. This elegant stone structure collapsed and was replaced in the 1960s by a more modern equivalent. The new bridge was built downstream from the original and the road from Monzievaird was re-routed. Strowan was an important market in the area when agricultural labour was hired for the new term. The old Cross was removed to Crieff and the adjoining church of Strowan (now a ruin) ceased as a centre of worship when the parish of Strowan linked with neighbouring Monzievaird in the early days of the nineteenth century. The view from the east shows Baird's Monument on Tom a chastel, the hill which is reputed to have been the site of the royal castle of Strathearn.

The present Drummond Arms is a Victorian building. It replaced the older one, where Bonnie Prince Charlie held his 'Council of War' some two weeks prior to the disaster of Culloden. The old building was called 'Drummond of Perth's Arms, Inn, Tavern and Hotel'.

Opposite below: Innerpeffrey Castle. The castle, to the east of the historic library of Innerpeffrey, lies in a magnificent setting on the banks of the Earn. Built in the sixteenth century for the Drummond family, it is now in ruinous condition, having apparently deteriorated over the last century. *Historic Scenes of Perthshire*, published in 1880 (Charles Alexander, Dundee) states, 'It is now a roofless ruin; but its walls with a staircase, and some of its apartments, are yet in a state of almost entire preservation'.

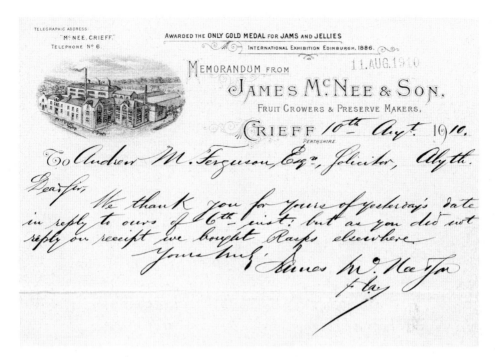

TELEGRAPHIC ADDRESS
"MCNEE, CRIEFF."
TELEPHONE No 6.

AWARDED THE ONLY GOLD MEDAL FOR JAMS AND JELLIES
INTERNATIONAL EXHIBITION EDINBURGH. 1886.

11. AUG. 1910

MEMORANDUM FROM

JAMES MCNEE & SON.

FRUIT GROWERS & PRESERVE MAKERS,

CRIEFF 10th Augt 1910.
PERTHSHIRE.

To Andrew M. Ferguson, Esqr, Solicitor, Alyth.

Dear Sir,
We thank you for yours of yesterday's date in reply to ours of 6th inst. but as you did not reply on receipt we bought Rasps elsewhere.

Yours truly
James McNee Son
& Co

Above: Soft fruit growing in Strathearn resulted in the development of a prosperous jam works. As can be noted from this 'memorandum', this old established company had a sizeable presence in the Bridgend. The building is still there, having been converted into homes by Hillcrest Housing Association and thus breathing new life into this historic part of the town.

Madderty Kirk, a delightful little country church located not far from the ruined pre-Reformation Abbey of Inchaffrey. The parish is somewhat unique in that, apart from St Davids, it has no villages. St Davids is of comparatively modern construction, having been erected by the proprietress Lady Campbell Preston as a memorial to her late husband Sir David Baird, the distinguished soldier. The village was erected on the site of Craig, a free burgh of Barony from an older period.

Located in the centre of the old village is the old building of Dunning, first mentioned in the charters of the Abbey of Inchaffrey Abbey in 1219, and dedicated to St Serf, a popular local saint. 'Many of the columns bear the characteristics of Norman architecture, whilst the small windows in the tower and the rounded arch over the doorway behind indicate Saxon workmanship'. (Marshall's *Historic Scenes of Perthshire*, 1880)

Right: Another of Strathearn's ancient churches, which is similar in style and age to St Serf's in Dunning. Muthill was a collegiate church which prior to the Reformation came under the See of the Bishop of Dunblane. The tower is reckoned to be the oldest part, dated by some as early as the ninth century. The elegant main church was built by Ochiltree, Bishop Dunblane in the early part of the fifteenth century. The old church has recently undergone extensive reparatory works under the auspices of Historic Scotland and is well worth visiting.

Below: Muthill Kirk at the end of the nineteenth century. One hundred years ago, the old Kirk was sadly neglected. The walls were covered in ivy which, although giving it a pleasant air of historical decrepitude, played havoc with the fabric.

Old Church, Muthill

Published by J. Ford Balfour, Comrie St.

37

A fine example of an eighteenth-century residence in the historic village of Muthill. Renovated some years ago, it now houses the Muthill Museum.

Muthill has a number of Georgian properties dating from around the early 1800s, most of which are around Highlandman Park. The castellated Little Culdees in Willoughby Street to the east of it incorporates many stones from the ruins of nearby Culdees Castle. This elegant portico is on Pitkellony Street.

Above and below: A cottage in Willoughby Street. No wonder the village has won awards in 'Perthshire in Bloom'! Summer now sees the village come to life in a blaze of colour from the floral displays. Baskets adorn the buildings and open spaces, giving it an almost continental atmosphere in high summer. Many of the old cottages and houses in the village have been restored from earlier neglect.

One of Strathearn's historic jewels, Drummond Castle dates back to 1500 and is the seat of the ancient Drummond family. The estate extended at one time as far as Callander and is extensive even now. Visited by Victoria and Albert on their 'Highland Tour', it featured more recently in the film *Rob Roy*.

The Italian gardens of Drummond Castle in around 1920. These beautifully maintained gardens are a feature not to be missed.

A 1906 photograph of this country house, located on the Culdees Estate on the edge of the village. It was demolished later in the last century. It was probably situated close to the older Culdees Castle. The Culdees were part of the old Celtic or Pictish Church, which held sway in Strathearn prior to the coming of St Columba. Their monastery, dating back to around the sixth century AD, was located in Muthill. It was possibly near to the castle which bore their name.

Hidden amongst the trees and unseen by the passing traffic, the Abbey of Inchaffrey in Madderty is one of the Strath's oldest buildings. Founded in 1199 by Earl Gilbert, second Earl of Strathearn, it was dedicated to the honour of God, the Virgin Mary and St John the Evangelist. The name is from the Gaelic and means in English the 'Isle of Masses', the ground being at one time surrounded by the Pow Burn. It was an Augustinian house and friars made their way across Strathearn and from further afield, bringing pastoral comfort to the local populace. Sadly, the ravages of time and the pillaging of its stones over the centuries have left merely a solitary gable and a small vaulted roof. In pre-Reformation days the Abbot was a powerful man, and indeed it was Abbot Maurice of Inchaffrey who gave Mass and blessed Bruce's troops before the Battle of Bannockburn in 1314. The Abbey failed to survive the Reformation and was partially destroyed by fire when being used as a private residence in the seventeenth century.

Above: Glen Artney Kirk. Located a way up the Glen, this little church was erected in the late nineteenth century by the Willoughby D' Eresbys, successors to the Drummonds of Drummond Castle. The church has a peaceful serenity and thankfully is still functioning on selected Sundays, when the minister from Muthill takes the service.

Left: The Little Kirk, Ramsay Street. Not all church buildings are or were as grand as those erected by the Victorians north of the High Street in Crieff. Crieff's ecclesiastical history is filled with stories of disruption and secession, not untypical of most small towns in Scotland in the eighteenth and nineteenth centuries. The 'Little Kirk' is featured in Porteus's *History of Crieff*, and still stands, although generally it is better known as the Red Cross Hall. Built in 1822, it was the church of a group of dissident Presbyterians who broke away from the 'antiburghers', who in turn had broken away or seceded from the established kirk over patronage or the right to appoint a minister. It was used as a temporary school when the present primary school was being built in 1876.

No wonder the old Parish Kirk seems to be absent from the numerous postcards of Crieff that were published in the last century! When the new church was built in Strathearn Terrace in 1882, this old building began its route down the slide of neglect. The glass in the windows of the tower has been vandalised, the roof has been retiled in asbestos cement slates now covered in a heavy moss growth, the stonework has been harled in a drab roughcast and the Local Authority removed half of the gravestones to 'tidy things up' some ten years ago. It does, however, fulfil a useful function as a community hall on a shoestring budget. It was built in 1787 on the site of an older church, which probably dated back to well before the Reformation. Interestingly, when it was demolished in the eighteenth century, forty gold coins from the reign of Robert the Bruce were discovered hidden in a wall.

This picture appeared in Porteous's *The History of Crieff*, now long out of print. The old school or parish clerk's house was located in the grounds of the old parish church. Its foundations are still there, above the wall in Bank Street. In 1726 it was rebuilt and became the parish school. The parish school moved to Commissioner Street, the site of the present Crieff Primary School, in the 1780s, where, as Porteous describes, a 'harled and whitewashed building was erected'.

Left and below: The 1780s building proved inadequate for the increasing number of pupils, so it was demolished and this attractive stone-built school (left) was erected in its place in around 1856, with a headmaster's house attached. Although the house was later demolished, the school was retained and its distinctive façade can still be clearly identified in the picture below.

Published by J. Ford Balfour, Comrie Street

The school was extended in around 1874, after the new School Board came into existence. The headmaster's house was demolished. Whilst the work was carried out the pupils were housed in the 'Little Kirk', now the Red Cross Hall in Ramsay Street. This picture shows the boys and girls were kept apart by a stone wall, and dates from around 1880.

44

This picture was probably taken in around 1910 and was included in Porteous's book, published in 1912. Since that date, the school has continued to grow, and has been extended as demand has increased. With the construction of Crieff High School, what had been Crieff Junior Secondary became Crieff Primary School.

The old toll house, Dollerie Terrace, one of the few remaining examples left of the toll houses that were erected at the beginning of the nineteenth century to implement the Turnpike Acts that Parliament had introduced to finance their road programme. This particular building was rescued from advancing decay in the 1980s when local builders J. & R. Robertson carried out extensive renovations.

The old Crieff Hospital in Pittenzie Street. The old 'cottage hospital' was around until comparatively recently, being made redundant when a replacement was erected on the site of the old railway sidings in King Street. Now demolished, it has made way for retirement flats, perhaps indicative of the dominant age bracket in the town today.

The new health centre in King Street, built on the site of the old coal yard of the railway station and opened in 2002. The building was required to support the town's growing population, replacing a smaller, inadequate centre next to the hospital. The extensive yards and sidings that were once part of the town's railway infrastructure have now largely been replaced by community buildings, such as the hospital and health centre, as well as a small industrial estate.

An elegant example of an early stone-built property renovated by local developer George Buchanan in the 1990s in King Street, opposite the Market Park. Many of these properties in this part of the town housed families of hand-loom weavers when linen and subsequently cotton weaving dominated the town's economy.

Across the Strath from Crieff lies the picturesque little village of Dunning. It is a place which breathes the past. This renovated, traditionally built stone cottage is reckoned to be the sole survivor of the 1714 uprising when Jacobite forces, retreating from their 'victory' at Sherrifmuir, torched a number of Strathearn towns and villages as part of the incompetent Earl of Mar's scorched earth policy.

Lochearnhead Hotel in the 1950s. Lochearnhead Hotel, at the junction of the A85 Crieff and the A84 Glen Ogle roads, was a busy tourist centre run by the Cameron family, headed by well-known Highland Games star Angus Cameron. It was destroyed by fire in the 1960s and the site is now occupied by residential housing. The 'new' Lochearnhead Hotel lies further to the east.

The hotel some two decades before. In the 1930s, the hotel was a favourite place for the well off, who drove up from the central belt to 'take tea'. Parking was altogether more casual, with the uniformed chauffeur standing in the middle of the road awaiting his employer.

The Amulree Hotel, an old eighteenth-century coaching inn on the River Braan, north of the Sma' Glen. It was a popular place for Crieffites and visitors to 'take tea' of a Sunday afternoon. This 1920s view is prior to the extensions being added.

The Amulree Hotel after the Second World War. Barely recognisable as being the same hotel as in the previous picture, the old inn has been harled and extensions added. Amulree lies on the tourist route to Dunkeld or Aberfeldy and has an ancient connection with the Celtic Saint Mael Rhuba.

Dundurn Church, St Fillans, one of three churches ascribed to St Fillan. The saint died here in AD649 and his body was transported up Glen Ogle. A violent dispute arose as to which of the two chapels dedicated to his name should inter the body, when suddenly there appeared not one but two coffins! Both sets of worshippers departed, content with a coffin each.

Grampian Hills Hydropathic. Once a popular hotel fronting onto the Comrie Road, it was burnt down in the 1950s and replaced with a modern style bungalow called Balmennoch.

Sealladhmohr Private Hotel
VICTORIA TERRACE   -   -   CRIEFF

Beautifully Situated.   Fine View.

Near Bowling Green and Golf Course.   Also
within short radius of famous Gleneagles Golf
Course. 10 Minutes from Station.

Mrs. A. S. HUGHES.
'Phone 127.   Miss H. S. PORTEOUS.

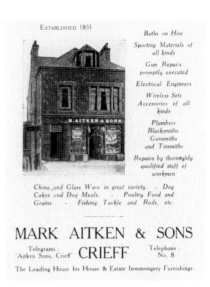

ESTABLISHED 1851

Baths on Hire

Sporting Materials of
all kinds

Gun Repairs
promptly executed

Electrical Engineers

Wireless Sets
Accessories of all
kinds

Plumbers
Blacksmiths
Gunsmiths
and Tinsmiths

Repairs by thoroughly
qualified staff of
workmen

China and Glass Ware in great variety. - Dog
Cakes and Dog Meals. - Poultry Food and
Grains. - Fishing Tackle and Rods, etc.

MARK AITKEN & SONS
Telegrams :   Telephone :
'Aitken Sons, Crieff' CRIEFF   No. 8

The Leading House for House & Estate Ironmongery Furnishings

Left: Sealladmohr, Victoria Terrace. This substantial property was a private hotel in the 1930s, as advertised in *Smith's Guide* of the time. Now a private residence, it is perhaps indicative of the changes in the local tourist trade over the last half century.

Right: Mark Aitken & Sons, House and Estate Ironmongers. This advert from *Smith's Guide to Crieff* (1930s) illustrates what a jack of all trades it must have been, trading as electrical engineers, plumbers, blacksmiths, gunsmiths and tinsmiths. You could even hire a bath! The building by the Tourist Offices in the Town House is now the Cancer Research Shop.

Methven Castle in 1905, since which time the castle has seen a transformation. The neglect of centuries has been halted as the Murdoch family, local architects, have organised its rehabilitation. Its elevated position to the east of Methven makes it eye-catching for miles around. The original castle was the home of the Mowbrays, a Norman family who settled in Scotland, becoming Earls of Methven. It eventually came into the possession of the Royal Stewarts and had a dramatic history. In the seventeenth century it was purchased by Patrick Smyth of Braco. The castle is about 300 years old.

Above: Mitchell Street, once a weavers' colony. For almost one hundred years, hand–loom weaving of linen and then cotton dominated the Crieff economy. At one time, some forty per cent of the working population derived their livelihood from the loom or kindred trades. Areas of the town were almost exclusively occupied by weavers, including Mitchell and Miller Streets above the Cross. Some of their cottages survive, having been modernised to provide comfortable homes.

Old Mill, Crieff.

Described on this 1918 postcard as 'An old mill, Crief', the subject was, in fact, the old generator producing power for the Crieff Electricity Supply Company. Located at Dallerie, adjacent to Morrisons playing fields and just south of the now removed embankment, the wheel was powered by the laid, which at one time flowed through here.

Opposite below: The Weavers' Hall in Commissioner Street. Sadly, the original structure was rebuilt in the 1930s and turned into flats. The weavers dominated Crieff life for more than a hundred years after the departure of the Tryst. The Crieff Weavers' Society was the oldest of the Strathearn Weavers' Societies, having been founded in 1768. The hall was built shortly afterwards and became a focal point in local activities. It was rented out to various groups and individuals for meetings, weddings, dances and musical soirees. It was at one time a place where cock fighting, the area's most popular sport, took place before being banned by the Society in the early 1800s along with the meetings of the local badger baiters. The hand-loom weavers suffered from the national economic decline of the industry after the Napoleonic Wars, and the Society was wound up in 1857. The census returns indicate the presence of hand-loom weavers in the town right up until 1891, but by then they were all retired.

Crieff High School under construction, 1960s. Looking south from Pittenzie, Crieff High School's skeletal frame takes shape. The High School provided Secondary Education to sixth form level. Apart from Morrison's Academy, which at that time provided placements for local pupils, Crieff Junior Secondary in Commissioner Street (now the primary school) provided education up to third form level.

Morrison's Academy, 1904. Founded in the mid-1800s by a Muthill builder, the school was originally to have been built in Muthill, but ended up in Ferntower Road in Crieff. The separate boys' and girls' schools amalgamated in the 1960s. It has increasingly attracted overseas boarders as the pattern of education has changed. Its status, too, has changed in the last half century. Once a blend of local, non-fee-paying pupils, as well as boarders and others from outside the immediate area, it became 'grant aided' and then totally independent. The main building stands in an elevated position overlooking the town.

four

Rover Moot

THIRD WORLD ROVER SCOUT MOOT AT MONZIE CASTLE NEAR CRIEFF
A GROUP INCLUDING ROVERS OF ALL THE 40 NATIONS REPRESENTED AT THE MOOT
PHOTO THE SCOTSMAN

The 1939 Rover Scout Moot held at Monzie Castle. As war clouds gathered over Europe, an event took place at Monzie Castle, near Crieff, which proved to be the last occasion the Boy Scout movement were to come together in a happy, carefree gathering of like souls before the world changed forever. Forty-two nations were represented at Monzie. They camped in the grounds of this delightful Perthshire estate from 16–26 July 1939, a mere five weeks before war was declared. This photograph shows representatives of all of the forty-two countries attending, not just from the 'British Empire', but from Europe, excluding Germany, and farther afield. The Scouts arrived by train at Crieff Station, at the foot of King Street, and were bussed the two miles to Monzie at the entrance to the Sma' Glen. The name 'moot' is apparently of Anglo-Saxon origin, meaning a meeting place. It was suggested by the founder of the movement, Baden Powell, as a suitable term for the scouting assemblies such as that held at Monzie.

Left: The procession winds its way into the grounds of Monzie Castle, the home of Mr D. Maitland Makgil Crichton, the local laird. This photograph was taken by one of the servants from the roof of the castle. The backdrop to the campsite was the steep slope of Kate McNivens's Crag, where an unfortunate lass of that name was executed as a witch in the seventeenth century.

Opposite below: The official camp site. The tented village laid out in the grounds of Monzie Castle was a favourite visiting place to visit of the local population, especially at the weekends, when buses were laid on from Crieff.

The march of the Scouts in front of Lord Somers, Deputy Chief Scout. This was a splendid sight, with over 4,000 Scouts involved. The eleven days of the Moot were blessed with fine weather. The 'march past' saw the countries pass by the saluting base in alphabetical order, led by Armenia and Belgium. In these pre-war days the sun had not yet set on the British Empire, and so the next contingent was an amalgam of the many countries that made up that large body of different races and religions. The *Strathearn Herald* of the period makes great play of the small contingent of Rovers from Lichtenstein, led by their own Prince Emanuel. They caught the eye with their colourful costumes and white stockings as they saluted the dais. Another contingent to draw attention were the Hungarians, whose goose stepping, pre-outbreak of war, did not apparently attract any approbation from the assembled multitude.

The platform was, as befits the age, strongly male orientated. Apart from Lord Somers, the Chief Scout, there was also John Colville MP, the Secretary of State for Scotland; Lord Rowallan (later to be Chief Scout in a post-war Britain); Prince Gustav Adolf of Sweden; and Col A.C. Johnstone, the Moot organiser.

The Scots Rovers pipe the haggis, carried by Mackenzie Ramage.

Iraqi Scouts at Monzie. Research into the internationalism of this unique gathering, taking place virtually at the onset of one of the worst wars in the history of humanity, makes interesting reading. Here we see a picture of one of the Iraqi Scouts who, during their brief sojourn in Perthshire, entertained the milling throngs of curious visitors. The *Strathearn Herald* reports that they enthralled the crowd with their 'Dervish dances'.

Polish Scouts at Monzie. It is somewhat ironic to look at the picture of the proud young Polish Scout smiling for the camera virtually days before his country was overrun by Nazi forces. Today we have a good number of people of Polish descent living in and around Monzie, descendants of Polish soldiers who fought on the side of freedom, and perhaps descendants of that unknown Scout camping on the innocent fields of Monzie.

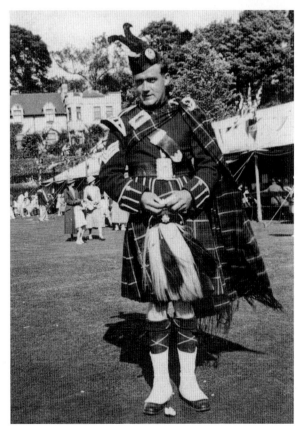

Peter McGregor, piper to the Laird of Monzie. Peter was a local Gilmerton boy and, apart from being the piper to the Laird of Monzie, doubled up as official piper to the Moot.

The Indian Rovers. The international nature of the Moot is illustrated by this turbaned Indian Rover Scout at the entrance to the camp.

Peter McGregor posing with the be-kilted dummy who was thrown from the battlements of the castle each morning as an 'old Scottish tradition'.

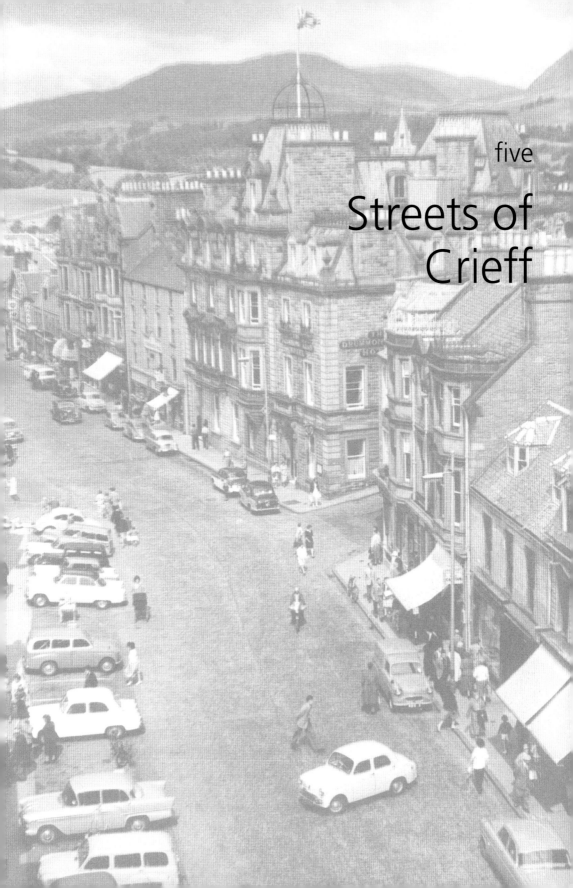

five

Streets of Crieff

Comrie Street, 1920s. This 1920s busy but traffic-free scene shows the wide variety of shops that Comrie Street offered at the time. Although the post office had moved to High Street, there was Speedie, the chemists, and below the Masonic hall McKenzie's 'haircutting rooms with shampooing and shaving saloons', in lieu of today's estate agents!

The War Memorial, Comrie Road. Erected at the junction of Burrell Street and Comrie Road after the First World War, this scene from 1924 shows the field guns placed on either side of the memorial. They are no longer there.

The Thistle Inn, East High Street, 1905. East High Street had two well-established inns after the First World War, The Crown (now sadly derelict and something of an eyesore) and the Star Inn (now the Crieff Hotel). Earlier there was, however, another inn. The Thistle Inn was run by J. Young and was on the other side of the road from its two rivals. Here we see the brewers' drays unloading more supplies to quench the thirst of the drouthy east-enders! The Thistle Inn was located where Baird's Buildings are now.

The foot of King Street, early 1920s. Not a lot of change in eighty years, apart from the trees at the 'Chains' which have now gone, and there are not many carters to be seen doing their rounds these days!

Burrell Street in 1925 – again we see what life was like before the reign of the motor car. The car, in the middle of the highway, ploughs its way up an untarmacked highway towards Burrell Square. The building on the right is the Meadow Inn, whilst the 1½-storey cottages on the left below the present Ard Howe Guest House have had major surgery to their upper parts, with the addition of non-traditional dormers.

Burrell Street, about 1900. Compared with the previous 1925 scene, there are not many changes in the buildings. The milk cart is making a delivery to a stone cottage which occupies the site of Derek Halley's Garden Centre. The children play in the street further up the road, unaware that the automobile is soon to change things dramatically.

Top of Burrell Street, about 1910, from the top of the street near its junction with the Comrie Road. The little girl is Elizabeth Fraser, who lived with her sister at No. 6 Burrell Square until the 1980s.

Burrell Square 1926. This elegant part of the town was constructed, originally on the west side, in the 1820s, and was known as the Octagon. Fine examples of interior Georgian design with panelled doors and simple plaster cornices are still retained in some.

High Street, 1904. Again, the buildings have not altered that much although the shops are of a different world.

James Square in 1856. According to the late Bob Torrens, whose excellent little book *Crieff in the News* appeared in 1991, this very old photograph was the work of two photographers, Henderson and Downie. They based themselves in Crieff for a short period with a studio in King Street displaying 'photographs and calotypes'. Bob tells us that the photograph was taken in 1856, making it the earliest known street scene of the town we have. It shows the extent of the weekly market which was held at the old Cross, opposite what is now Church Street. The building on the right-hand side was 'Willie Brydie's House', probably built before 1700 and demolished in 1869.

James Square in the early part of last century. In the fifty years that have elapsed since the first photograph was taken differences are appearing. Some gas lighting can be seen outside the 'Drummond', and the Murray Fountain is in place.

The top of Ferntower Road leading to the Hydro in 1907. Despite the passage of nearly 100 years, not a lot has altered, with the exception perhaps of the traffic! Ferntower was the line taken by Wade when constructing his military road after the 1714 uprising.

St Margarets or College Buildings, one of the most distinctive buildings in Crieff, built by a Dr Malcolm of Madderty to house students some 200 years ago, the building's fortunes have fluctuated over the years. It was a girls' seminary until cholera hit, and was for a number of years home to many of Crieff's weavers, the home of the rector of Morrison's Academy and a police station and prison! Today, part of the building is a hotel and the rest flats.

High Street, Crieff, from the Town Hall clock tower. Crieff man David Cowan used some family influence to gain access to the old clock tower of the Town House and take this panoramic view of the High Street in the pre-yellow-line era of the 1960s.

six

A Strathearn Miscellany

The Michaelmas Fair was historically the most looked-forward-to event for Crieff's citizens. The fair, held in October, coincided with the Tryst, the great cattle market when some 30,000 cattle arrived in the environs of the town from all the airts accompanied by the tartan-clad drovers. The fair continued after the demise of the Tryst and the main driving force seemed to be the hand-loom weavers of the town, who had organised themselves into an effective Guild in the late 1700s. Stalls were set out from the Cross, right down to where the Market Park is now situated, offering a wide variety of goods. This picture, taken by McFarlane, one of the town's leading Victorian photographers, shows two worthies enjoying a drink together and dressed for the occasion.

The Tryst and the black cattle. Pictured near Lochearnhead, this is a descendant of one of the beasts which made the trip from Skye to Crieff in the 1980s as part of a television programme on the Tryst. The cattle were not all black, but came in a variety of shades and colours, including the more common dun or brown.

The old Arms of Crieff, although largely regarded as a thing of the past with the changing pattern of local government, do tell an interesting tale. Adopted by the Town Council as the official seal, they were described thus in a publication of 1898:

ARMS OF CRIEFF

> The seal is emblematic of historic scenes in the district. In pre-historic times the Earls of Strathearn – scions of the Royal family – had their stronghold on Tomnachastel, a conical hill some three miles south west of Crieff. The earls were succeeded by the Stewards of Strathearn who held courts in a field about a mile from the town on what is now part of the Broich Estate. The stayt or skeat where the court was held was about 12 yards in diameter with the centre raised and on which the Earls or Chief Judges sat. The seal represents the Earl sitting upon the mound dispensing justice. On the left is the Cross of Crieff. In the fore ground are the Crieff iron stocks or jougs which are still seen at the door of the court House and are almost the only remains of this kind in the country.

The jougs referred to, together with the old Cross, are now displayed in a room below the Tourist Office in High Street.

Roman Camp, Entrance to Sma' Glen, near Methven

The Roman occupation of the third century AD saw the construction of the impressive Gask Ridge forts, the oldest Roman frontier known, and stretching from Ardoch near Braco to Bertha at what is now Inveralmond. The Romans also built Glen Blockers at Dalginross in Comrie and Fendoch at the entrance to the Sma' Glen. The latter proved an interesting excursion for the Victorian residents and holidaymakers to Strathearn. Although obscured in the summer months by bracken, the fort can still be seen clearly at other times.

The well-known Scottish water colourist, John Patrick Downie RSW (1871–1945), who trained at the Slade and in Paris, gained fame as a painter of interiors as well as Scottish fisher folk. This painting shows the old tower of the twelfth-century Muthill Kirk and the traditional housing of the village. (Information from Christine Aiton of Aiton Fine Arts, Crieff)

The Dog Head Well, Muthill, around the time of the First World War; an interesting relic of yesteryear located on the road beside Highlandman Park in the ancient village of Muthill. It was here that the drovers would stop on their way south to the Falkirk Tryst to water the beasts and take a short rest.

Thornhill Street, Muthill, 1903. The approach into Muthill was by 'Wade's Road', as it was then known, and the Highlandman Park.

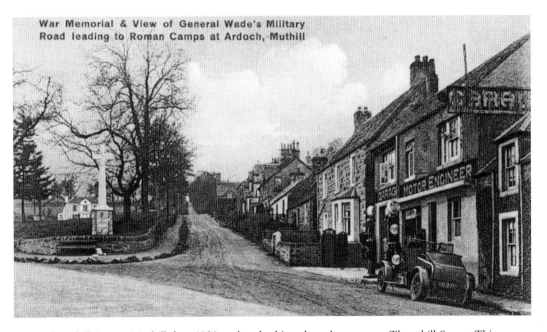

Thornhill Street, Muthill, late 1920s, taken looking the other way up Thornhill Street. Things have changed since then, but the garage is still a garage.

Drummond Street, Muthill, in 1904. Whilst the buildings have not changed much in appearance over one hundred years, the number of shops in Muthill has declined to virtual extinction. The people of the village in the 1900s had more than a dozen stores serving their needs, including boot makers, grocers, butchers and newsagents. Here, on this side of Drummond Street, you can pick out three shops plus the Commercial Inn.

The Square and Old Cross, Fowlis Wester, 1904. Fowlis has retained a serene air despite the passage of time. Originally, the old Perth Road went through the village. When the present lower route was built the village became somewhat sheltered from the passage of time. The square housed the Pictish Cross, which was moved inside the nearby church, and a replica put in its place.

The Fowlis Inn. The old inn set further back from the Square is now a private residence. This photograph is about the time of the First World War.

The school and other houses at Monzievaird, about three miles to the west of Crieff, about 1910. The school is long since closed, the nearby church is demolished and the little community hall is under threat. New families have, however, moved into the old estate houses built in the nineteenth century by the Murrays of Ochtertyre, and so they give us hope for the future.

Above and left: David Cowan dramatically captures the mood of the Comrie Flambeaux in his 1960s pictures. Comrie has preserved one of the oldest New Year's ceremonies still extant in Scotland. The Flambeaux comprises a procession headed by torch bearers who visit the various corners of the village, followed by costumed children and young people. The Flambeaux is replicated in other parts of Scotland. According to older tradition, as recorded in Drake-Carnell's book *It's an Old Scottish Custom* (Peter Davies; London, 1939), the 'shopkeepers and housewives lay in a good stock of cakes and fruit and, even if the original Hogmanay cake, a kind of sweet bread, is not universally baked ready for the advent of the guisers, still there are few houses which fail to respond to the children's demands'.

Get up, gude wife, and bin no sweir
And deal your cakes and cheese, while you are here
For the time will come when you'll be deid
And neither need you're your cheese nor breed

The Comrie ferry boat. Prior to the 'new' bridge at Dalginross, intrepid travellers could cross the Earn by ferry. These were 'rope ferries', with the boatman pulling on the rope stretched across the water. Similar ferries to this were found at one time at Innerpeffrey and at Caputh on the Tay.

The Earthquake House, Comrie, 1908. Comrie, known as Scotland's earthquake village, sits on the Highland Boundary Fault Line and has experienced tremors of various magnitudes over the centuries, the first recorded in 1597. The most severe shock was in 1839 when walls were cracked and chimney pots fell down. The Comrie Pioneers were founded at that time by postmaster Peter MacFarlane and shoemaker James Drummond, who devised an early 'scale of intensity'. A seismoscope, designed by Peter Mallet, was placed in the little Earthquake House, built in 1869, which has the distinction of being the smallest historic building in Europe!

Left and below: Floods in Comrie about 1909. The 1990s saw concern about the flood risks in Comrie. The problem had manifested itself in the early 1900s, as can be seen by the flood waters in Dalginross and the River Earn.

Opposite above: A Masonic procession on its way to the official opening of Comrie Primary School, about 1910.

RIVER EARN IN FLOOD AT COMRIE.

Below: MacRosty Park has been for over a century a favourite place for both locals and visitors to relax and enjoy the scenic charms of Strathearn. Originally a nursery, it was bought by James MacRosty, a well-known solicitor and former Provost who gifted it to the town. It has witnessed many changes over the decades. The Victorian bandstand still stands, although sadly somewhat redundant compared with previous years. The Tea Rooms visible in the postcard have been demolished, as changing tastes and maintenance costs sounded their death knell half a century ago. The mill lade which was such a pleasant feature dried up after damage to the weir at the north end of the park was never made good.

Macrosty Park in the 1920s. Family groups picnic under the shade of the park's magnificent trees.

Snowbound James Square in the 1960s. Prior to the Square being completely altered in the 1990s, traffic to King Street passed on either side of the Murray Fountain.

Fire at Bank Street in 1962. A dramatic picture showing the aftermath of the fire, which destroyed Gilbert's Warehouse in Bank Street, next to the old parish church.

Jimmy Stewart, known as the 'Cock o' the North', was a character seen often around Crieff in the 1960s. An ex-soldier, he chose to live as did. It is said that the stick in his right hand was in fact a scabbard for a weapon of steel, a probable deterrent to any would-be assailants!

Crieff and District Ambulance Service in 1945. The wartime effort of many Crieff citizens saw service not only in the armed forces but the auxiliary services, such as ambulance and fire. The town and surrounding area was an important staging post for many troops, and Scots, English and Irish, as well as Canadian and Polish regiments, found themselves based in Strathearn.

An Edwardian tea on the lawn in Crieff, 1903. The McLeish family of Croftmorag (now Findal) in Victoria Terrace, or George Street, as it was once known. Maid Janet Bowden serves up whilst members of the family relax on the front lawn. The summer house or gazebo on the right-hand side was a pre-requisite of garden furniture in an era when the automobile and the garage were still new toys. The advent of the railway brought an influx of people to the town and many fine stone dwellings similar to this one appeared north of the High Street from about 1880 onwards.

Sir Alex Douglas-Home, MP and Prime Minister. In 1963, Sir Alex Douglas-Home resigned his peerage when chosen to be Prime Minister by the incumbent Conservative Party. A convenient by-election had been called in the Kinross and West Perthshire and Sir Alex was given a clear run when the youthful George Younger, the incumbent Tory candidate, stood down. Much of the campaign was fought in and around Crieff and, with such a nationally and internationally known person involved, media interest was high. Comedian Willy Rushton, standing as an Independent, drew much attention, but Sir Alex triumphed with a majority of over 9,000 votes. Some twenty-five or so years later, things had changed when the resurgent SNP captured this traditionally Tory bastion in a hard-fought campaign caused by the death of the flamboyant Nicky Fairbairn.

Above and below: Eppie Callums' Tree, one of Crieff's landmarks. The oak tree is very old and features in a number of tales over the years. One assertion that the 'Great Montrose' hid amongst its leafy limbs is geographically out by a good three or four miles – the tree in question was adjacent to the now demolished Inchbrakie House. Eppie Callums' identity has been lost in the mists of time, but legend states that she planted an acorn in a tea pot and from that small beginning this giant oak tree has grown. These pictures, taken about the turn of the last century, show the tree set amidst a truly rural background. There was at one time a small ale house here, frequented by the drovers on their way to Crieff Tryst. History repeated itself when the Oakbank Inn, a modern building now a private residence, traded on the site in the 1980s.

Eppie Callums' Tree, as it is now. Still standing, the old tree now looks over a bustling residential suburb of the town. Although surrounded by modern houses, the Turretbank area is still rural with the parks on one side and Lady Mary's Walk on the other.

Glen Turret distillery and the Famous Grouse. Glen Turret is the oldest operating distillery in Scotland. It has been a prominent feature over the centuries, from a time when whisky was distilled illegally in the hills about Crieff. Today the Famous Grouse Experience attracts tourists by the bus-load, coming to enjoy a wee dram and watch the skilled processes involved in whisky production.

Above and below: Another two McFarlane photographs, both very faded, showing the formal opening of Crieff's new reservoir at Culcrieff, to the west of the Knock near to where the Hydro (Culcrieff) golf course is now located. The opening was performed by Mrs Finlayson, wife of Provost Finlayson, on 29 April, 1903. Apart from this good lady, the occasion seems to have been a bit of a men-only occasion!

Glen Artney, a Royal deer forest. For centuries the Stewart Kings of Scotland hunted deer in the forested slopes of the Glen. In 1842 Prince Albert, husband of Victoria, enjoyed stalking the stag during their stay in Strathearn. Sir Walter Scott wrote in *The Lady of the Lake*,

The stag at eve had drunk his fill
When danced the moon on Monan's rill
And deep his midnight lair had made
In lone Glenartney's hazel shade

The Glen, alas, is now greatly depopulated. The school closed in the 1950s and many of the little cottages like the one pictured here now lie deserted. The native Perthshire Gaelic of its long-gone inhabitants is sadly now hushed.

David Cowan captures a fine study of one of the area's many standing stones on the high moors south of Comrie. There are five close by one another on Dunruchan Hill. Other stones are to be found scattered throughout the Strath, and they date back to the Neolithic period, 3,500BC.

Steaming on Loch Earn in the 1920s. For many summers charabanc and train trips took visitors
and locals from Crieff and other parts of Strathearn to the attractive little village of St Fillans at the
eastern end of Loch Earn. The steam vessel *Queen of Loch Earn* plied the seven or so miles down to
Lochearnhead, a trip that must have been a real joy on warm summer days. It was owned and run
by Crieff entrepreneur Peter Crerar.

The old post office at St Fillans. At the end of the nineteenth century, the pace of rural life in the
pre-automobile era was so gentle. Here we see the distribution of parcels outside the old post
office, as locals gathered around for a 'wee blether', and to pass the time of day!

Although the motor car was just becoming part of the rural scene, this 1920s picture of Lochearnhead village paints a different picture.

Motoring in the early days. This sylvan avenue between Crieff and Muthill is somewhat busier now than it was in those peaceful days preceding the First World War.

Above: There is no date to the photograph of this procession down East High Street. It appears to be about 1910, judging by the fashion and the troop of Boy Scouts who can be seen directly behind the brass band. The Scout movement started in 1908, so this Crieff troop must have been amongst the earliest founded in this part of Scotland.

Left: Procession up East High Street, probably in the 1930s. Regrettably, we are unable to identify the date and indeed the reason for this march up East High Street, passing what is now Chic Brock's chip shop. Most marches tended to come from the other direction. It might have been to do with the unemployment issues of the time, although the all-male ensemble look quite cheerful with straw boaters to the fore.

Local businessman and First World War historian Bob Holsman identifies this as probably the 6th Volunteer Battalion of The Black Watch parading with pipes and drums down East High Street, past what was Bob's shop! The Drum Major leading the parade is P. McNeil of Perth, who died in action some few years later. The Battalion were at camp at Monzievaird in 1913.

The Black Watch on parade before the First World War. This extensive military parade enters Crieff from the east on the Perth Road and is seen passing the old Episcopal Church (now demolished) and Taylor's Institution School. The size of the contingent is considerable. Again, Bob Holsman identifies these men as the 6th Battalion, The Black Watch (Territorials). They were probably on their way to their annual camp at Monzievaird.

17th Lancers parade down East High Street, 1906. It is not quite clear why this cavalry regiment (known as the 'death or glory boys') was parading down East High Street; it may have been a recruiting drive or perhaps an involvement with the Games. By coincidence, the author's grandfather was serving in the regiment at this time. They had served in the Boer War and been involved in the relief of Mafeking.

Dewars was a plumbers shop located near what is now the Crieff Video Shop. The shop is bedecked for the festivities of George V's coronation in 1910. In the pre-television and radio era, enthusiasm for such events seemed to overcome the political turmoil and affiliation of the area, the roots of which lay in the far-off days of the eighteenth-century uprisings.

The Jesus Well at the foot of the Knock. Constructed in 1874, the Jesus Well has been for many years a favourite Sunday stroll for Crieff residents. The biblical inscription regarding the waters of life seem to have lost a little of their impact as there has now been erected an official sign advising people of the unsuitability of taking a drink from the bowl! The young lady with the hat pictured in 1907 seems quite unperturbed by any such risk!

Edwardian ladies in Crieff. These young ladies enjoy a stroll along one of the paths on what is possibly Lady Mary's Walk. The date is about 1905. The Walk was formed in 1815 by Sir Patrick Murray of Ochtertyre. His daughter Lady Mary often enjoyed the peaceful ambience of the path as it followed the course of the Earn tumbling its way eastwards from Comrie, and it was after her that the Walk was formally named.

The Kind Gallows of Crieff, recalled by Sir Walter Scott in *Old Mortality* and by the historian MacAulay, dominated the mound at Gallowhaugh and caused the Highland drovers coming to the Tryst in the eighteenth century to doff their bonnets in superstitious respect as they passed by with their beasts. When no longer required in 1746, they were removed and fell into the possession of James Wright, who ran a smiddy at the top of King Street. Part of the gallows was used as a lintel to a window in his property and drew much curiosity. When the building was demolished and the police station built in its place, James Wright's coat of arms was saved and built into the new front façade.

The cairn memorial to Maggie Wall near Dunning. The area of Glen Devon achieved much notoriety in the seventeenth century, when a succession of witch trials saw a number of helpless souls condemned and burnt as witches or warlocks. One such hapless person was a young lass called Maggie Wall, who was condemned and executed in 1657. This cairn was erected by unknown locals and is kept in good order by 'persons unknown'.

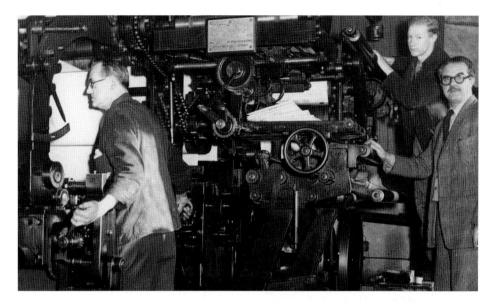

For many years the *Strathearn Herald* was a family-operated business, run by the Philips family for many generations from their Comrie Street premises. In the days prior to computerised-technology the paper was produced on their vintage Cossar press. This picture, from around 1970, shows printers David Cowan and Tom Lawson with editor David Philips snr, meeting a deadline.

Crieff Co-op in East High Street, about 1912. The Co-op was where Di Marco's shops and yard are now located. In the photograph are van man Andrew Graham and the baker Mr McKenzie. The bake house was at the top of the yard behind the amusement arcade.

A line up of Crieff Co-op employees about 1912 lined up outside the bakery in what is now Di Marco's yard in East High Street. The manager William Forsyth is pictured back row, second right, with the flat cap.

This is a fine study of Andrew Graham, who made the deliveries for the Crieff Co-op, taken before the First World War. In the pre-motor era, deliveries were made by horse and cart. Andrew is seen holding the horse brushes.

The McKenzie family of Crieff, about 1910, posing in their Sunday best. Mr McKenzie was the Co-op baker in East High Street.

A Crieff highland dancer. Highland dancing was a popular interest for many of Crieff's younger citizens. This portrait, taken about 1910, shows Miss McKenzie, pictured with her family above, in her competition gear.

Above: Inglis Garage at the Cross, early 1930s. No longer a garage, this building became Arcus House, the Crieff Co-op drapers, before being converted in the early 1980s into flats and shop units. The site has seen many changes over the years. At one time it was Coull's the fishmongers and prior to that even housed a small circus with a dancing bear! The old hay loft to the rear is still there.

Left: A tinkers' dispute in East High Street, Crieff, outside Miss McGregor's Laundry. Crieff and the surrounding district has for many years attracted a large number of travelling families, or tinkers as they were referred to in days gone by. They worked on the 'tatties' in the autumn months and had little problem finding temporary work

This boating scene, opposite Castle Cluggie on Ochtertyre Loch, was taken in 1906. The castle is of great antiquity; it was described as long ago as 1467 in a Murray charter as being 'an ancient fortalice'. It was supposedly one of the strongholds of the Red Comyn, the rival to Robert the Bruce who was killed by him at the Convent of Minories in Dumfries.

Bathing in the Earn, 1920s. This was a popular spot opposite the Braidhaugh for a summer splash in those days before recreation centres came into fashion.

PORTEOUS HALL, CRIEFF

FLYING VISIT—For One Night Only

THURSDAY, NOVEMBER 20th, at 8-0

ADMISSION (including tax) : Numbered Seats, 3/6 ;
Unreserved 2/4 and 1/2

Early Door 7-15 6d. extra ; Ordinary 7-50 ; Commence 8-0

N.B.—2/4 Tickets purchased in advance admit by the early
door without extra charge.

Tickets at F. Simpson, Stationer, 10–11 James Square

J. BANNISTER-HOWARD

PRESENTS

CECIL BARTH'S Company, in

'Charley's Aunt'

By Brandon Thomas

From the GARRICK THEATRE, ROYALTY THEATRE
LONDON OPERA HOUSE, etc

Screams of Laughter from Start to Finish

BOOKING OFFICE NOW OPEN

SECURE YOUR SEATS EARLY

Left and below: 'Charley's Aunt' plays Crieff in the 1920s. In the days before television, travelling theatre companies played rural towns throughout the country on one-night stands. Here is an advert circulated in the 1920s for a performance in the Porteous Hall with 'J. Bannister-Howard presenting Cecil Barth's Company' in this popular play of the times. Charges ranged from 1/2 (about 6p) to 3/6 (18p) for tickets. You could get admitted fifteen minutes early by paying an extra 6d!

100

Right: T.F. McFarlane was one of the town's earliest photographers, who called himself a 'photo artist'. He had a studio in King Street in the centre of the town, but lived with his family in a new villa in Ferntower Road. The stern subject of his portrait is unknown but bears a passing resemblance to Queen Victoria! This was around 1890.

Below: Fancy dress parade in Crieff about 1913. The reason for the occasion is not clear, but the town enjoyed a number of these self-entertainment fun days, no doubt a tradition borne of the Michaelmas Fair which at this time was beginning to fade away.

Crieff Public School about 1917–18; this was Infant 1 with their teacher Miss Clarke. The building in Commissioner Street still serves as a primary school, although prior to the opening of Crieff High School it functioned as a Junior Secondary, which took pupils up to the end of the third year.

The local Home Guard, pictured outside the Drill Hall in Meadow Lane, who despite a Dad's Army connotation performed a valuable role in the early days of the war when equipment comprised a few ex-Morrison's Academy Cadet Corps', Lee Enfield rifles from the earlier confrontation.

A deserted High Street, Auchterarder, in the early 1900s, before the car took over. The Lang Toon was once known as the town of many bridges on account of the stone slabbing laid over the water courses or strands that ran down both sides of the street, as shown in the photograph.

The Cross, Auchterarder, 1900s. Auchterarder was once an ancient Royal Burgh and its history reflects its important past. The ancient castle of Auchterarder was reputedly one of Malcolm Canmore's favourite stopovers when hunting in the Strath. The town grew with the linen and cotton industry and, when hand-loom weaving went into decline, numerous power-loom factories sprang up by the Ruthven water.

Blackford from the churchyard. Blackford, once a prosperous brewing and distilling village, suffered when these industries fell upon hard times. Its key location next to the A9 has facilitated a revitalisation. The demand for bottled waters and the locating of Highland Spring in the village has proved an economic benefit.

Monzie in 1900. Monzie was the main village in the parish before Gilmerton developed. It was a halting place for drovers coming down the Sma' Glen for the Crieff Tryst in the eighteenth century. The Statistical Account of the period indicated that their presence was not always welcome, as they were not averse to helping themselves to the tatties in the fields and the cottagers' possessions!

A tranquil and idyllic Gilmerton in the early 1900s.

The road out of Gilmerton, 1906. The pony and trap pass one of the traditional cottages that are found in this part of Strathearn. Many were originally heather thatched, but were eventually slated.

Waid's Road. As part of the Hanoverian strategy to diffuse political tension in the Highlands after the 1714 uprising, General Wade, an Irishman to boot, was put in charge of a road-building system between Crieff and Inverness. Much of the existing road through the Sma' Glen follows his route. This stretch, however, does not. It runs from Monzie northwards towards the Fulford Inn.

Buchanty 1907. Buchanty on the Almond is a small clachan famed for, amongst other things, its 'spout' and the leaping salmon, as well as its mispronounced usage in post-war Glasgow pantomimes!

Drumtochty at the turn of the nineteenth century. The little village of Drumtochty, or Harrietfield, as it is now known, nestles in the hillside above Glen Almond near Buchanty. Although some modern buildings now intermingle with the traditional, the village still retains the peaceful charm depicted in this picture taken at the end of the Victorian era.

Mid Lodge Monzie, about 1930s, a typical rural scene in pre-war Strathearn with the carter delivering his load. Mid Lodge Monzie Estate was built over the Shaggie Burn. The building has now been demolished.

Main Street, Methven, 1920, a Strathearn village which still retains much of its earlier character in the buildings along Main Street and Church Road. Methven features regularly in Scottish history back in the times of Wallace and Bruce.

Melville's Monument from Dalginross, about 1907. Dalginross was virtually an entity on its own for many years. The view looking up Glen Lednock shows Melville's Monument silhouetted against the skyline. Viscount Melville was a turbulent politician who as Henry Dundas rose to high rank in Pitt's administration. He was regarded by many as the Governor General of Scotland and made not a few enemies. He was impeached for reputedly misappropriating funds whilst Treasurer to the Navy, but was acquitted.

Front Street, Braco, about 1910. Braco is another of the attractive Strathearn villages which retains much of its early charm, as depicted in this 1910 picture.

Back Street, Braco, 1920. Braco has not changed a great deal since the 1920s in the village part, but has acquired a large number of new houses on its periphery.

The adverts placed in this 1860 tourist guide to Strathearn indicate that Crieff was already benefiting from the arrival of the railway. A wide range of shops provided locals and visitors alike with a range of services. Coals no longer had to be carted over the Ochils, but were delivered to coal depots like John Herron for local delivery.

The Commercial Inn was located in King Street and the somewhat fawning prose of Mr Alexander Stewart, the grocer, seems more than a little dated a century and a half later!

seven

Railways

Above: Highlandman Station in the 1930s. This evocative shot shows a teenage Margaret Kirkland from Dornock Farm awaiting the train to Crieff where she went to school. Margaret cycled the few miles from the farm and left her bike on the platform, awaiting her return later that day. The station is still there but is a private residence. The line crossed the road with level crossing gates. Margaret still lives in the area and is active in local matters. She was Chieftain of the Crieff Games some years ago.

The lines from Gleneagles Junction and Methven both approached Crieff from the east. Robbie's Box is the name of the cottage next to the original signal box which controlled traffic in and out of the town. The view looking due north towards Pittenzie and Croftnappock has changed dramatically since this 1950s picture. The fields to the left now house Crieff High School and the Recreation Centre, whilst those to the right have abandoned their agricultural purpose to provide yet more houses for the town's burgeoning population.

Opposite below: Highlandman Station. This was the last halt before Crieff. There was a level crossing on the up side of the line, whilst the approach to the station was from Muthill Station to the south. The line passed Strageath, crossing the Earn by a viaduct near Dornock Farm and into Highlandman. The picture shows that the station was not isolated. The buildings of the adjoining sawmill can be seen.

Above: Abercairney Station. A feature of the rural railway system in Strathearn was the large number of small, comparatively isolated stations on the route into Crieff. Abercairney Station lay south of Quarterbank Cottage, out with the curtilage of the estate. When the railways were constructed in the 1850s, many of the landowners subscribed to the share issues of the companies involved and often seemed to have a say in where many of these rural stations were located.

Above and below: Crieff Station before the First World War, *c.* 1908. Crieff Station had become the focal point of the local economy. It had a veritable hinterland of sidings and yards, cattle pens, timber mills and a coal depot. The Gleneagles Junction traffic, plus the later Methven Branch line, entered the station in parallel. The extension to Comrie and onto Lochearnhead had been completed by this time

Opposite below: Kildrummie Station, Methven, was on the Methven Branch Line which eventually connected Perth to Crieff, near to the present saw mill south of the village.

The foot of King Street at the entrance to the station in the early 1900s. The Comrie connection had opened in 1893, and the link to Lochearnhead in 1897, enabling traffic to link up with the main line to Oban through Glen Ogle and Dochart. Business was on the increase and one can see from this picture the number of people and the horses and carts gathered about the station entrance. The line extension caused not inconsiderable disruption, including the moving of the original station northwards, making a cutting through the Town Green (where the Somerfield supermarket is now), as well as tunnelling under Burrell Street and the area around Sauchie.

Crieff Station, prior to closing in 1964. Here is a British Railways passenger service getting up steam.

Abseiling on the Comrie Line in the 1960s. After the line closed, it was a number of years before the various bridges and viaducts were removed. Here an intrepid local takes the opportunity to perfect his abseiling technique on the viaduct over the Turret Burn.

Comrie Station, c. 1920s. Located to the east of the village, the caravan park is now situated on the station site.

Auchterarder Station. Like a number of Strathearn stations, Auchterarder was not actually located within the town, but over a mile away to the south east.

Railway Viaduct, Kincardine Glen Auchterarder. A fine example of Victorian engineering, still in use today.

Above and below: Lochearnhead Station. On the main line north to Oban, the Lochearnhead Station was for a while the meeting place for those coming from the east via Crieff and heading north through Glen Ogle to Crianlarich, and then north to Fort William or west to Oban.

This isn't a bad attempt is it.

The weather is rather broken, glad to hear you are going away on 20th.

Your Loving Nephew. Rob. A.

Above: Lochearnhead from above the Oban Line. Taken in 1906, this picture displays the grandeur of this lost line with the gentle curve of the viaduct as it sweeps up Glen Ogle.

David Cowan's study of a passenger train steaming up Glen Ogle above Lochearnhead on the Oban Line was taken shortly before the line closed to traffic. The line headed along Glen Dochart to Crianlarich and then westwards to the Atlantic shore line.

Opposite below: Greenloaning Station. The small community of Greenloaning had its station located on the main line between Perth and Stirling. It suffered, as so many did, with the Beeching axe falling in the sixties. In the last few years new housing developments have transformed this small community into a thriving body, with a good balance of both young and old.

Heavy snows in the 1920s. This dramatic scene between Gleneagles Junction and Crieff shows the efforts being made to keep the line open to traffic.

Crianlarich West Highland Station, the station on the route west to Oban. Passengers from Crieff and Strathearn connected with the line north from Callander at Lochearnhead for Oban.

eight

Crieff Hydro

Above: The Hydro as it looked in 1904. Opened in 1868, The Strathearn or Crieff Hydro is still under private ownership and has established itself as perhaps the finest family holiday establishment in Scotland, if not in the United Kingdom. Progressive changes and additions have kept the Hydro ahead in its field.

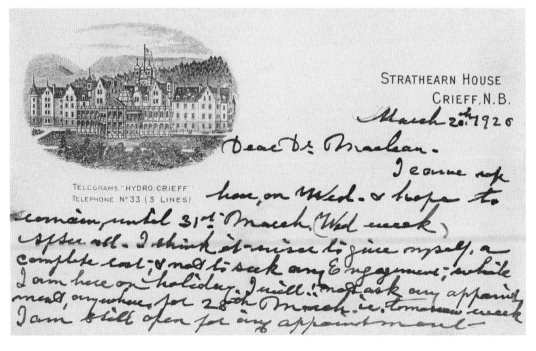

STRATHEARN HOUSE
CRIEFF, N.B.

March 20th 1920

Dear Dr Maclean,

TELEGRAMS "HYDRO, CRIEFF"
TELEPHONE Nº 33 (3 LINES)

A copy of the pre-First World War terms of the Hydro as shown in their history, published for their 125th anniversary.

CRIEFF HYDRO HOTEL 1868 – 1993

PRINTED EPHEMERA
❖ ❖ ❖ ❖ ❖ ❖ ❖ ❖ ❖ ❖ ❖ ❖ ❖

TERMS PER WEEK.

DURING JULY, AUGUST, SEPTEMBER,
Also 'Xmas, New Year and Easter Holidays, with Orchestra.

BOARD AND LODGING, one person £3 6 6
Two or three sharing same bedroom, each . . . 2 19 6
Children under 14 years (alone), £2, 5s. 6d. and £2, 2s. sharing.

MARCH, APRIL, MAY, JUNE, OCTOBER.

BOARD AND LODGING, one person £2 19 6
Those sharing 2 12 6
Children under 14 years, £1, 15s. and £1, 9s. 9d. respectively.

NOVEMBER, DECEMBER, JANUARY, FEBRUARY.

BOARD AND LODGING, one person £2 12 6
Those sharing 2 5 6
Children under 14 years £1, 9s. 9d. and £1, 8s. respectively.

For a long residence in Winter (November to February only),
the Ninth Week is Free.

Visitors for less than a Week, 1s. per Day extra.
Superior Rooms from 7s. to 21s. per Week extra.
Fire in Private Room, from 1s. 6d. per day ; Evening 9d.
Each Meal served in Private Room, 6d. extra.
Private Servants in Servant's Room, 4s. 6d. per Day ; if sharing with Visitor, 3s. 6d.
During July, August, September, 6d. per Day more.
Young Children taken by arrangement.

First Consultation Fee, 10s. 6d. Medical Attendance in Private Room extra.
Electric and Massage Treatment charged moderately. Other Baths Free.
No Gratuities.

ACCOMMODATION FOR PRIVATE HORSES, CARRIAGES, & MOTORS (Inspection Pit).
DOGS FORBIDDEN IN THE HOUSE. KEPT AT STABLES 2s. 6d. WEEKLY.

Accounts rendered Weekly up to Wednesday Morning.

During July, August, and September, accommodation should be secured before
coming, stating probable length of stay. Superior Rooms, if desired, cannot always
be guaranteed, but if such be not available on arrival, temporary substitutes are
provided. Before leaving, three days' definite notice is required, else such will
be charged. Visitors require to have their luggage packed and access given to the
room by noon, on the day of departure.

MEALS.

BREAKFAST, 8.30 (9 in Winter) ; LUNCH, 1.15 ; DINNER, 7.
Afternoon Tea. 4.15 ; Tea or Coffee after Dinner.
On SUNDAYS—BREAKFAST, 9 ; DINNER, 1.30 ; TEA, 5 ;
SUPPER, 8.30.

Family Worship after Breakfast, and 9.45 p.m. Sundays, 9 p.m.

Lights off Public Rooms at 10.50 p.m.; lowered in Lobbies at 10.45; Bedrooms at 11.

Address for Telegrams—"HYDRO, CRIEFF."
Telephone No. 33, Crieff.

... SHOWING THE WEEKLY TERMS.

PAGE 25

Opposite below: The Meenister's Recuperation. Crieff Hydro (short for hydropathic), like so many similar establishments throughout Scotland, was founded as a place where visitors could relax and 'take the waters'. This 1926 postcard shows how things have changed. The Hydro called itself Strathearn House and the address on the card is a nomenclature widely used at the time – 'Crieff N.B.' (North Britain!). The Hydro was built on ground once owned by the Church of Scotland, and traditionally ministers of religion receive a discount on the standard terms. Stress is not a new illness and the tone of the card sent to the Free Church Offices in Edinburgh reveals quite a bit. 'I came up here on Wednesday to remain until 31st March (Wednesday week). I think it wise to give myself a complete rest and not to seek any engagements.'

Above: The Winter Gardens, a popular feature of the Hydro, where guests could take tea under the shady palms.

Opposite above: The drawing room at the Hydro. This elegant room features a portrait of Sir David Baird by Raeburn. Baird retired from the army, having had a distinguished career under Wellington, and married Miss Campbell Preston of Ferntower. His monument dominates the landscape between Crieff and Comrie.

Opposite below: A 1954 family group enjoying the pleasures of the old Hydro pool, now replaced with a more modern model.

THE DRAWING-ROOM, CRIEFF HYDROPATHIC. 103

THE SWIMMING POOL, CRIEFF HYDROPATHIC. 105

Other local interest titles published by Tempus

St Johnstone FC
ALASTAIR BLAIR

On Tuesday 24 February 1885, members of the St Johnstone Cricket Club met to form a football club. Since that evening, St Johnstone FC has grown to one of the established names in the country, and Saints have been responsible for nurturing some of the greatest Scottish talents, including Sir Alex Ferguson, Ally McCoist and Sandy McLaren. This book is a celebration of all those who made a contribution to the team.
7524 2183 2

The Black Watch
LT-COL S.J. LINDSAY

The Black Watch Regimental Archives contain many thousands of photographs graphically illustrating the history of this famous Highland regiment since the first images were recorded some 150 years ago. Over two hundred of these pictures have been selected for this volume to represent different aspects of regimental life both at home and abroad, in peace and at war. The collection also covers the Territorial battalions of the Black Watch from early days as Rifle Volunteers through the two World Wars.
0 7524 1763 0

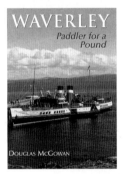

Waverley: Paddler for a Pound
DOUGLAS MCGOWAN

Waverley, the world's last sea-going paddle steamer, was destined for the scrap yard in 1974 when Douglas McGowan and the Paddle Steamer Preservation Society purchased her for the princely sum of £1 and the rest is, as they say, history. Fresh from a £7million refit in Great Yarmouth, *Waverley* is resplendent in her black, red and white livery and can be seen sailing the coast of Britain again.
0 7524 2877 2

Scotland's Malt Whisky Distilleries
JOHN HUGHES

In Scotland, between 1750 and the present day, over 700 distilleries have been legally registered to make single malt Scotch whisky. Less than ninety survive. Blighted by such factors as war, poor harvests, prohibition and mergers, those that have survived each have a unique tale to tell. From Glenturret to Arran, the history of every one of the surviving distilleries is told in this book.
0 7524 2592 7

If you are interested in purchasing other books published by Tempus, or in case you have difficulty finding any Tempus books in your local bookshop, you can also place orders directly through our website

www.tempus-publishing.com